Organizing Finances to
BUILD
WEALTH!

Bill Paying Organizer Book

Activinotes

DAILY JOURNALS, PLANNERS, NOTEBOOKS AND OTHER BLANK BOOKS

NAME: ....

ADDRESS: ....

CONTACT NOS.: ....

....

....

Month_____

Bills

INCOME
RENT
GAS
GROCERIES
LEFT FOR BILLS

EXPENSE	DUE	AMOUNT	PAID	BALANCE LEFT

NOTES

Month_____

Bills

INCOME
RENT
GAS
GROCERIES
LEFT FOR BILLS

EXPENSE	DUE	AMOUNT	PAID	BALANCE LEFT

NOTES

Priority Expenses for the month

- [ ]
- [ ]
- [ ]
- [ ]
- [ ]
- [ ]
- [ ]
- [ ]
- [ ]
- [ ]

- [ ]
- [ ]
- [ ]
- [ ]
- [ ]
- [ ]
- [ ]
- [ ]
- [ ]
- [ ]

APPOINTMENTS

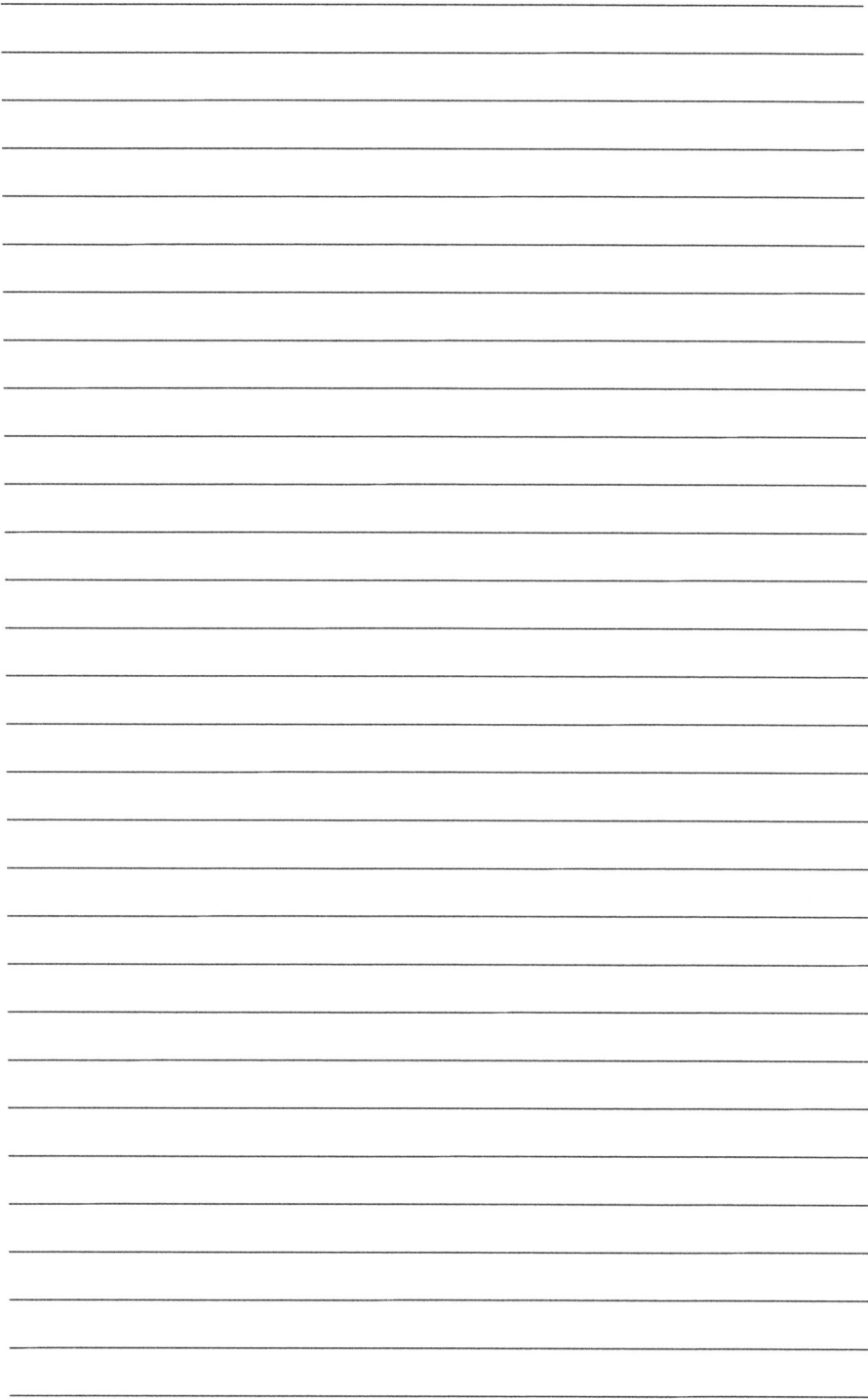

Month_____

INCOME
RENT
GAS
GROCERIES
LEFT FOR BILLS

Bills

EXPENSE	DUE	AMOUNT	PAID	BALANCE LEFT

NOTES

Month_____

Bills

INCOME
RENT
GAS
GROCERIES
LEFT FOR BILLS

EXPENSE	DUE	AMOUNT	PAID	BALANCE LEFT

NOTES

Priority Expenses for the month

- ☐
- ☐
- ☐
- ☐
- ☐
- ☐
- ☐
- ☐
- ☐
- ☐

- ☐
- ☐
- ☐
- ☐
- ☐
- ☐
- ☐
- ☐
- ☐
- ☐

APPOINTMENTS

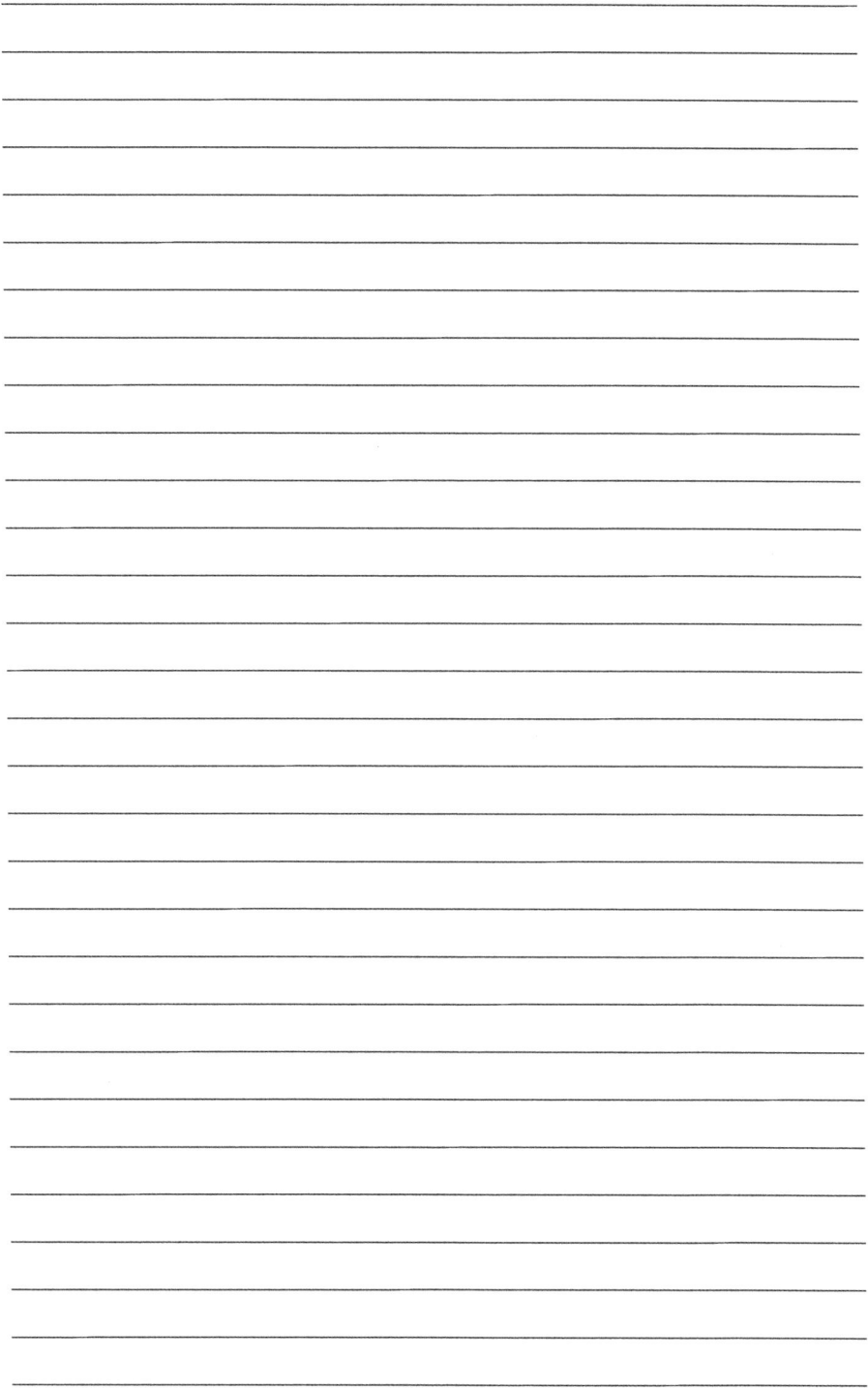

Month_____

Bills

INCOME
RENT
GAS
GROCERIES
LEFT FOR BILLS

EXPENSE	DUE	AMOUNT	PAID	BALANCE LEFT

NOTES

Month_____

Bills

INCOME
RENT
GAS
GROCERIES
LEFT FOR BILLS

EXPENSE	DUE	AMOUNT	PAID	BALANCE LEFT

NOTES

Priority Expenses for the month

- [ ]
- [ ]
- [ ]
- [ ]
- [ ]
- [ ]
- [ ]
- [ ]
- [ ]
- [ ]

- [ ]
- [ ]
- [ ]
- [ ]
- [ ]
- [ ]
- [ ]
- [ ]
- [ ]
- [ ]

APPOINTMENTS

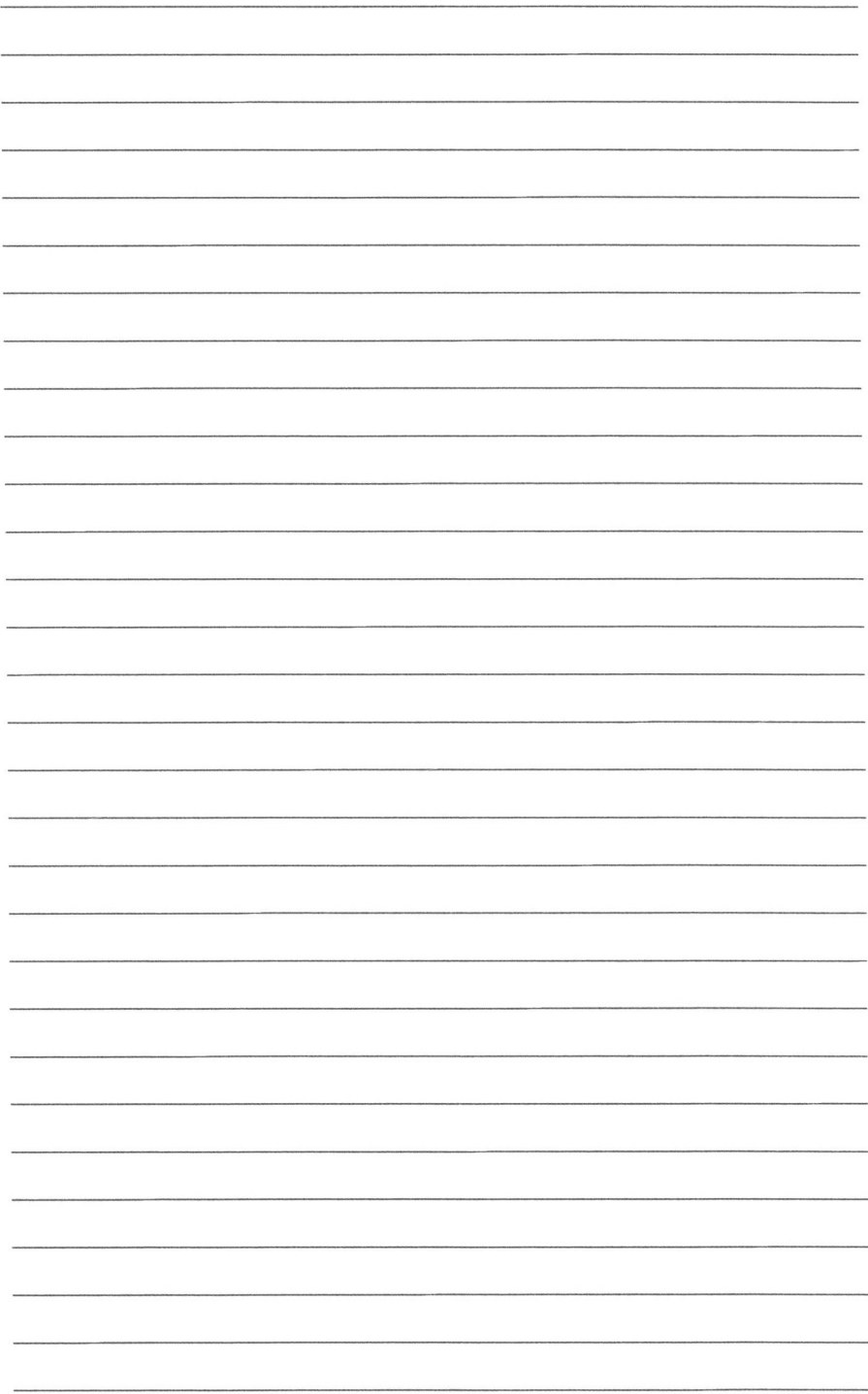

Month_____

Bills

INCOME
RENT
GAS
GROCERIES
LEFT FOR BILLS

EXPENSE	DUE	AMOUNT	PAID	BALANCE LEFT

NOTES

Month_____

Bills

INCOME
RENT
GAS
GROCERIES
LEFT FOR BILLS

EXPENSE	DUE	AMOUNT	PAID	BALANCE LEFT

NOTES

Priority Expenses for the month

- [ ]
- [ ]
- [ ]
- [ ]
- [ ]
- [ ]
- [ ]
- [ ]
- [ ]
- [ ]

- [ ]
- [ ]
- [ ]
- [ ]
- [ ]
- [ ]
- [ ]
- [ ]
- [ ]
- [ ]

APPOINTMENTS

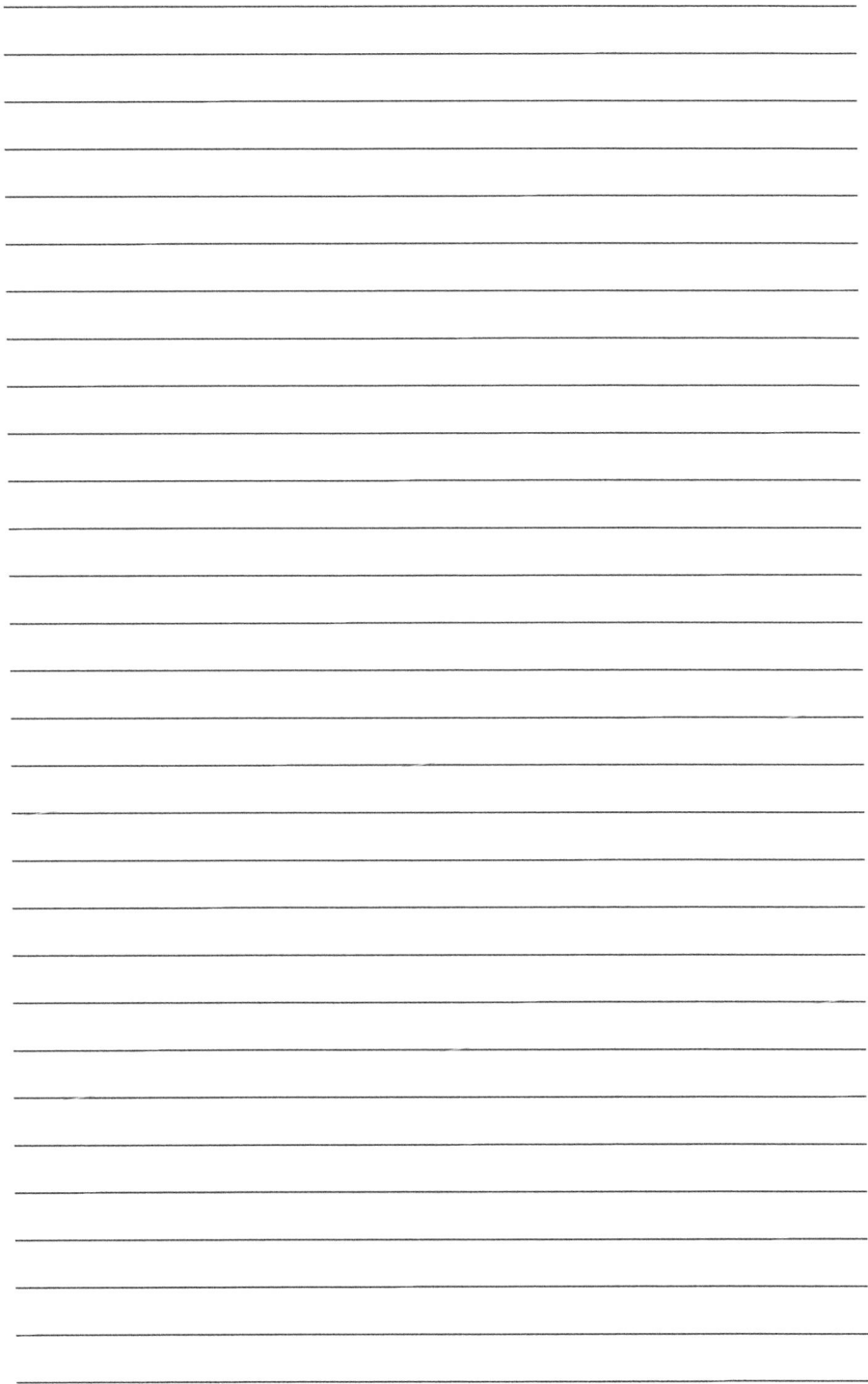

Month_____

Bills

INCOME
RENT
GAS
GROCERIES
LEFT FOR BILLS

EXPENSE	DUE	AMOUNT	PAID	BALANCE LEFT

NOTES

Month_____

Bills

INCOME
RENT
GAS
GROCERIES
LEFT FOR BILLS

EXPENSE	DUE	AMOUNT	PAID	BALANCE LEFT

NOTES

Priority Expenses for the month

- [ ]
- [ ]
- [ ]
- [ ]
- [ ]
- [ ]
- [ ]
- [ ]
- [ ]
- [ ]

- [ ]
- [ ]
- [ ]
- [ ]
- [ ]
- [ ]
- [ ]
- [ ]
- [ ]
- [ ]

APPOINTMENTS

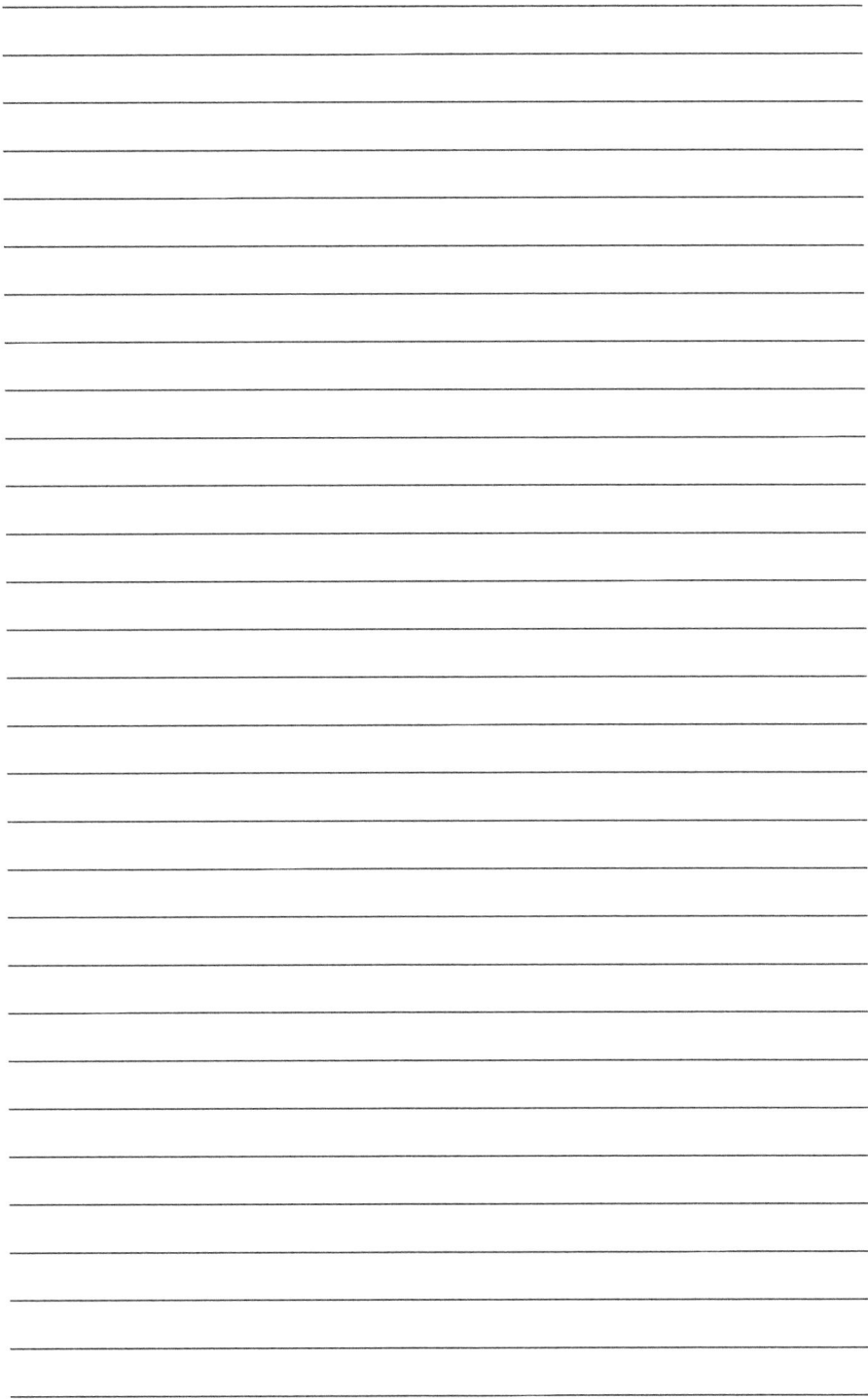

Month_____

Bills

INCOME
RENT
GAS
GROCERIES
LEFT FOR BILLS

EXPENSE	DUE	AMOUNT	PAID	BALANCE LEFT

NOTES

Month_____

Bills

INCOME
RENT
GAS
GROCERIES
LEFT FOR BILLS

EXPENSE	DUE	AMOUNT	PAID	BALANCE LEFT

NOTES

Priority Expenses for the month

- [ ]
- [ ]
- [ ]
- [ ]
- [ ]
- [ ]
- [ ]
- [ ]
- [ ]
- [ ]

- [ ]
- [ ]
- [ ]
- [ ]
- [ ]
- [ ]
- [ ]
- [ ]
- [ ]
- [ ]

APPOINTMENTS

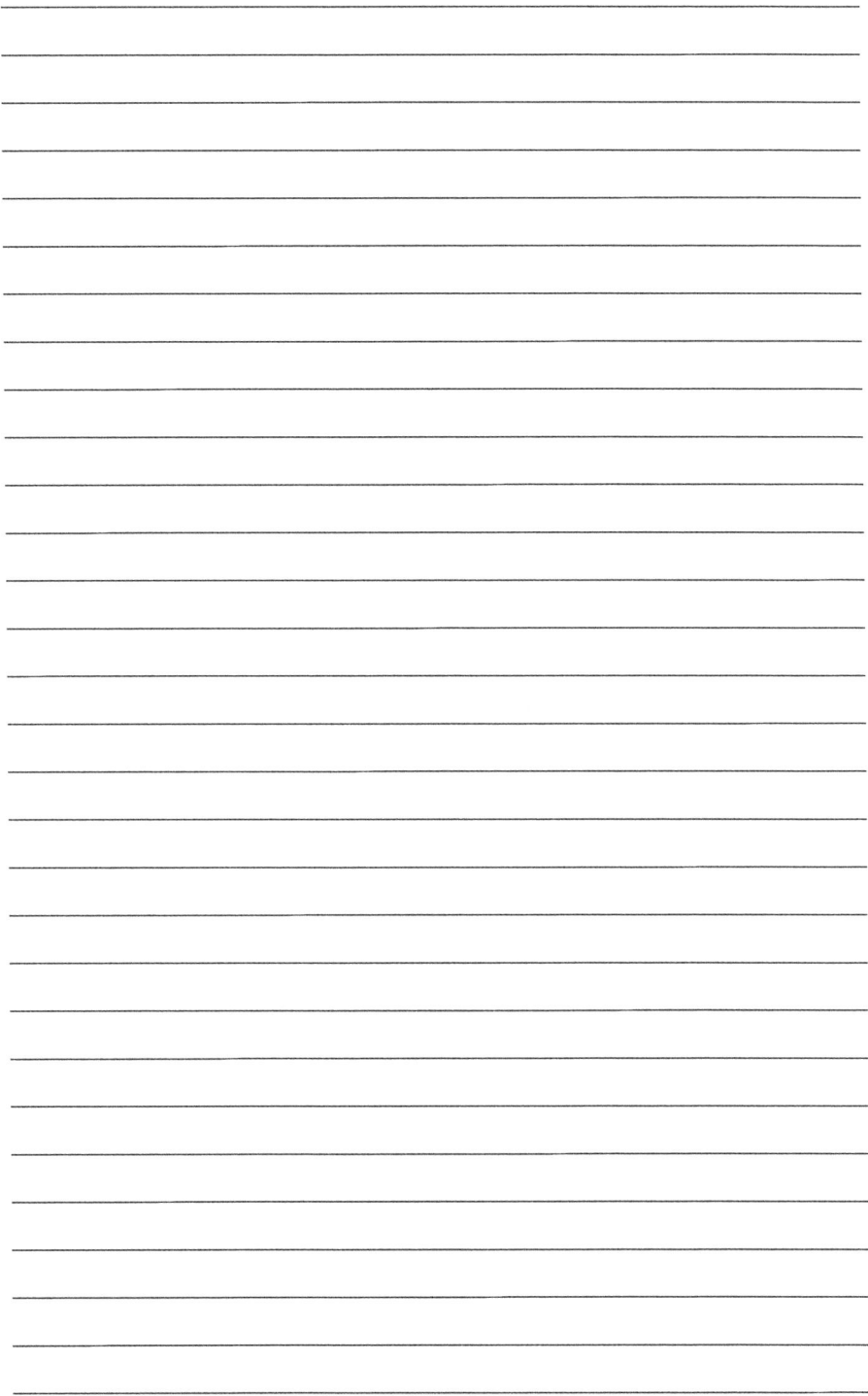

Month_____

Bills

INCOME
RENT
GAS
GROCERIES
LEFT FOR BILLS

EXPENSE	DUE	AMOUNT	PAID	BALANCE LEFT

NOTES

Month_____

Bills

INCOME
RENT
GAS
GROCERIES
LEFT FOR BILLS

EXPENSE	DUE	AMOUNT	PAID	BALANCE LEFT

NOTES

Priority Expenses for the month

- [ ]
- [ ]
- [ ]
- [ ]
- [ ]
- [ ]
- [ ]
- [ ]
- [ ]
- [ ]

- [ ]
- [ ]
- [ ]
- [ ]
- [ ]
- [ ]
- [ ]
- [ ]
- [ ]
- [ ]

APPOINTMENTS

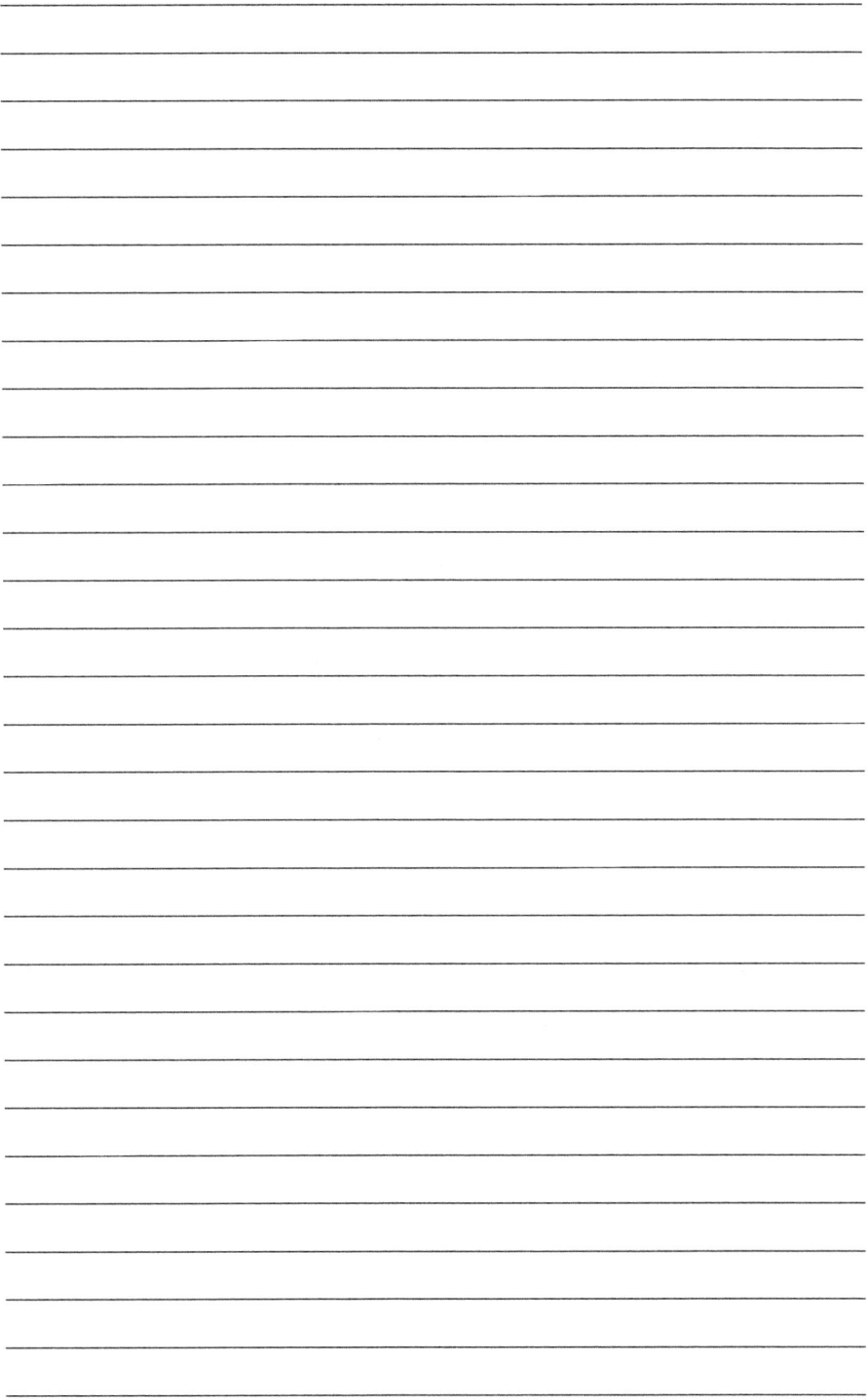

Month_____

Bills

INCOME
RENT
GAS
GROCERIES
LEFT FOR BILLS

EXPENSE	DUE	AMOUNT	PAID	BALANCE LEFT

NOTES

Month_____

Bills

INCOME
RENT
GAS
GROCERIES
LEFT FOR BILLS

EXPENSE	DUE	AMOUNT	PAID	BALANCE LEFT

NOTES

Priority Expenses for the month

- [ ]
- [ ]
- [ ]
- [ ]
- [ ]
- [ ]
- [ ]
- [ ]
- [ ]
- [ ]

- [ ]
- [ ]
- [ ]
- [ ]
- [ ]
- [ ]
- [ ]
- [ ]
- [ ]
- [ ]

APPOINTMENTS

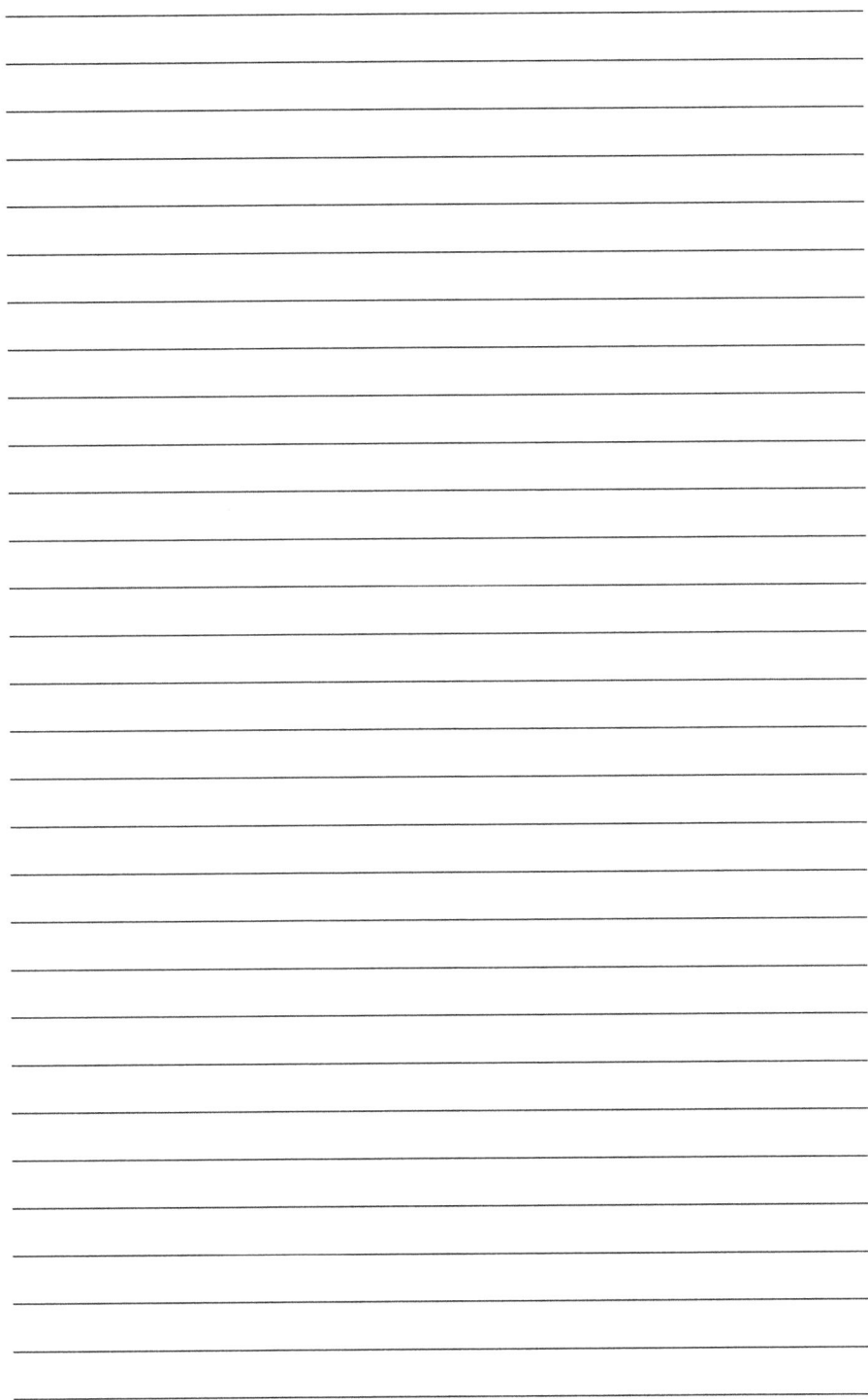

Month_____

Bills

INCOME
RENT
GAS
GROCERIES
LEFT FOR BILLS

EXPENSE	DUE	AMOUNT	PAID	BALANCE LEFT

NOTES

Month_____

Bills

INCOME
RENT
GAS
GROCERIES
LEFT FOR BILLS

EXPENSE	DUE	AMOUNT	PAID	BALANCE LEFT

NOTES

Priority Expenses for the month

- [ ]
- [ ]
- [ ]
- [ ]
- [ ]
- [ ]
- [ ]
- [ ]
- [ ]
- [ ]

- [ ]
- [ ]
- [ ]
- [ ]
- [ ]
- [ ]
- [ ]
- [ ]
- [ ]
- [ ]

APPOINTMENTS

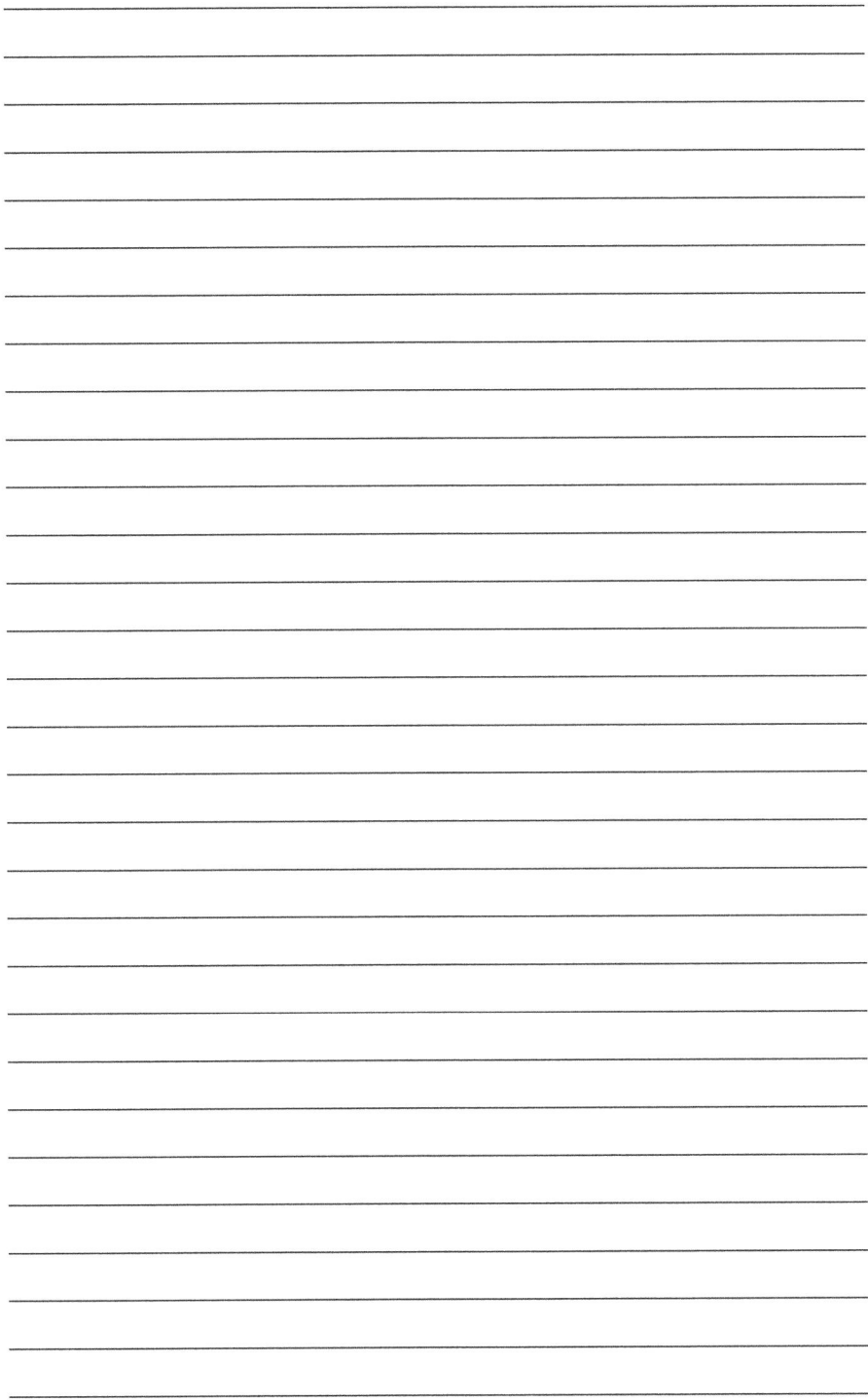

Month_____

Bills

INCOME
RENT
GAS
GROCERIES
LEFT FOR BILLS

EXPENSE	DUE	AMOUNT	PAID	BALANCE LEFT

NOTES

Month_____

Bills

INCOME
RENT
GAS
GROCERIES
LEFT FOR BILLS

EXPENSE	DUE	AMOUNT	PAID	BALANCE LEFT

NOTES

Priority Expenses for the month

- [ ]
- [ ]
- [ ]
- [ ]
- [ ]
- [ ]
- [ ]
- [ ]
- [ ]
- [ ]

- [ ]
- [ ]
- [ ]
- [ ]
- [ ]
- [ ]
- [ ]
- [ ]
- [ ]
- [ ]

APPOINTMENTS

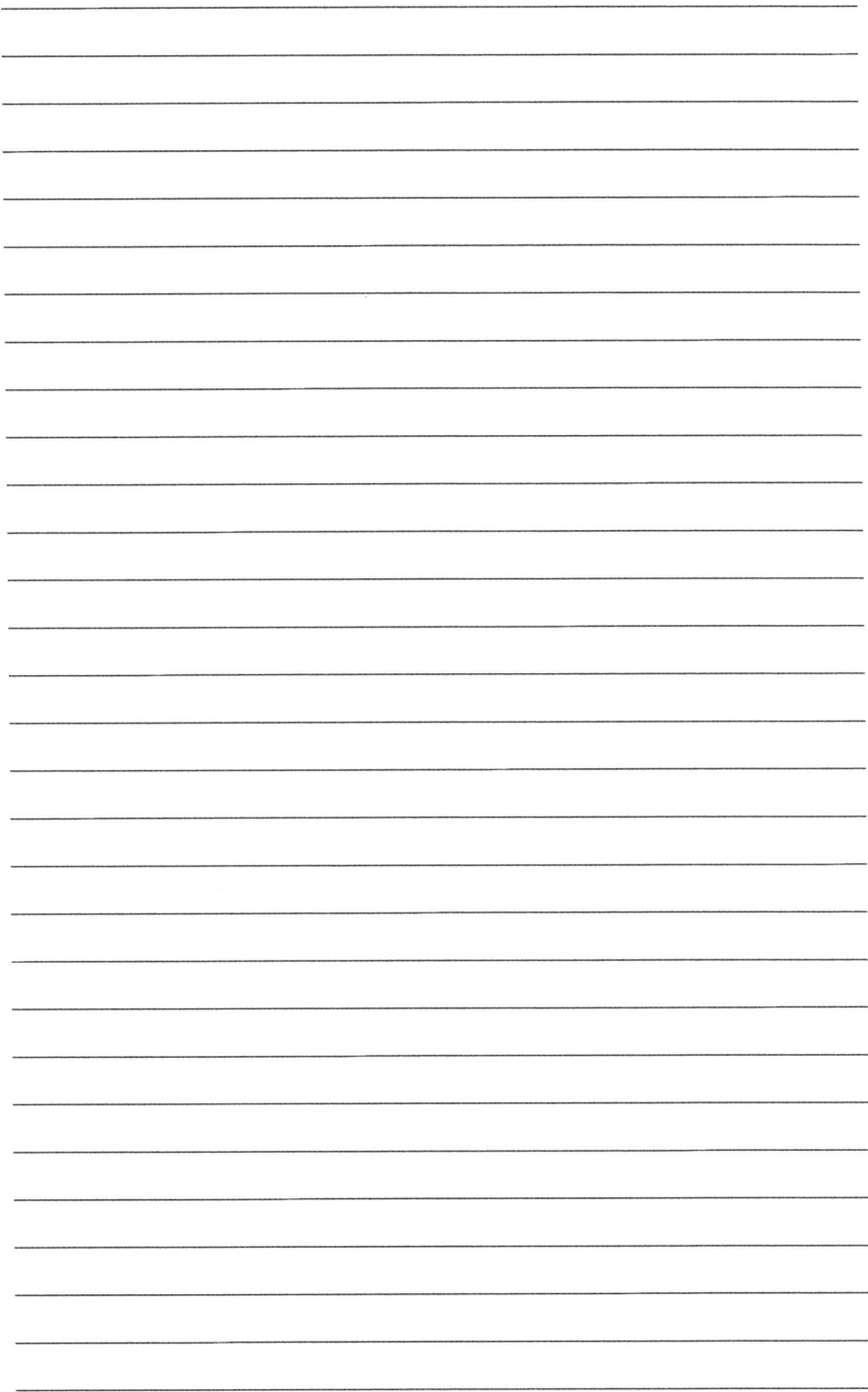

Month_____

Bills

INCOME
RENT
GAS
GROCERIES
LEFT FOR BILLS

EXPENSE	DUE	AMOUNT	PAID	BALANCE LEFT

NOTES

Month_____

Bills

INCOME
RENT
GAS
GROCERIES
LEFT FOR BILLS

EXPENSE	DUE	AMOUNT	PAID	BALANCE LEFT

NOTES

Priority Expenses for the month

- [ ]
- [ ]
- [ ]
- [ ]
- [ ]
- [ ]
- [ ]
- [ ]
- [ ]
- [ ]

- [ ]
- [ ]
- [ ]
- [ ]
- [ ]
- [ ]
- [ ]
- [ ]
- [ ]
- [ ]

APPOINTMENTS

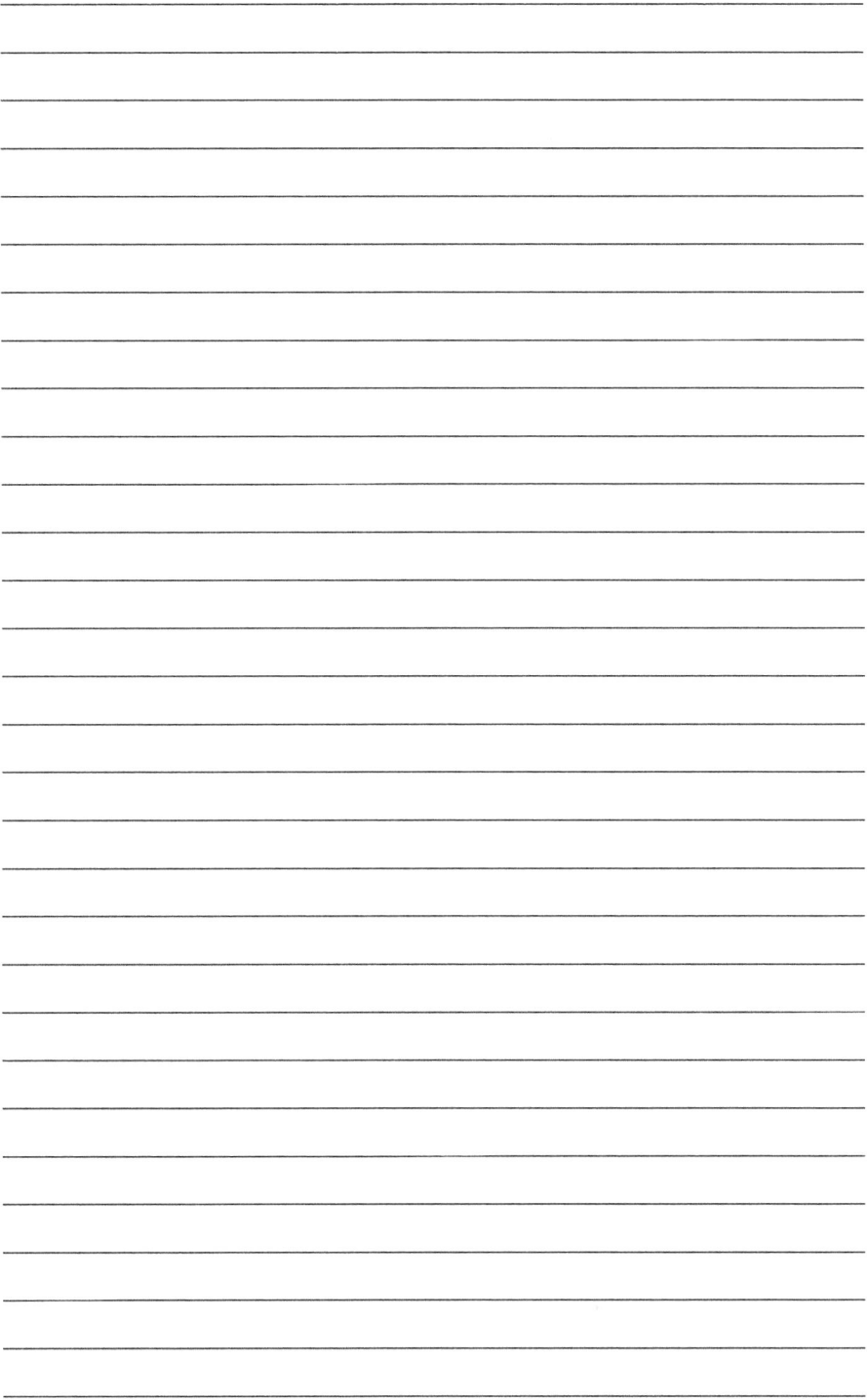

Month_____

Bills

INCOME
RENT
GAS
GROCERIES
LEFT FOR BILLS

EXPENSE	DUE	AMOUNT	PAID	BALANCE LEFT

NOTES

Month_____

Bills

INCOME
RENT
GAS
GROCERIES
LEFT FOR BILLS

EXPENSE	DUE	AMOUNT	PAID	BALANCE LEFT

NOTES

Month_____

Bills

INCOME
RENT
GAS
GROCERIES
LEFT FOR BILLS

EXPENSE	DUE	AMOUNT	PAID	BALANCE LEFT

NOTES

Month_____

Bills

INCOME
RENT
GAS
GROCERIES
LEFT FOR BILLS

EXPENSE	DUE	AMOUNT	PAID	BALANCE LEFT

NOTES

Priority Expenses for the month

- [ ]
- [ ]
- [ ]
- [ ]
- [ ]
- [ ]
- [ ]
- [ ]
- [ ]
- [ ]

- [ ]
- [ ]
- [ ]
- [ ]
- [ ]
- [ ]
- [ ]
- [ ]
- [ ]
- [ ]

APPOINTMENTS

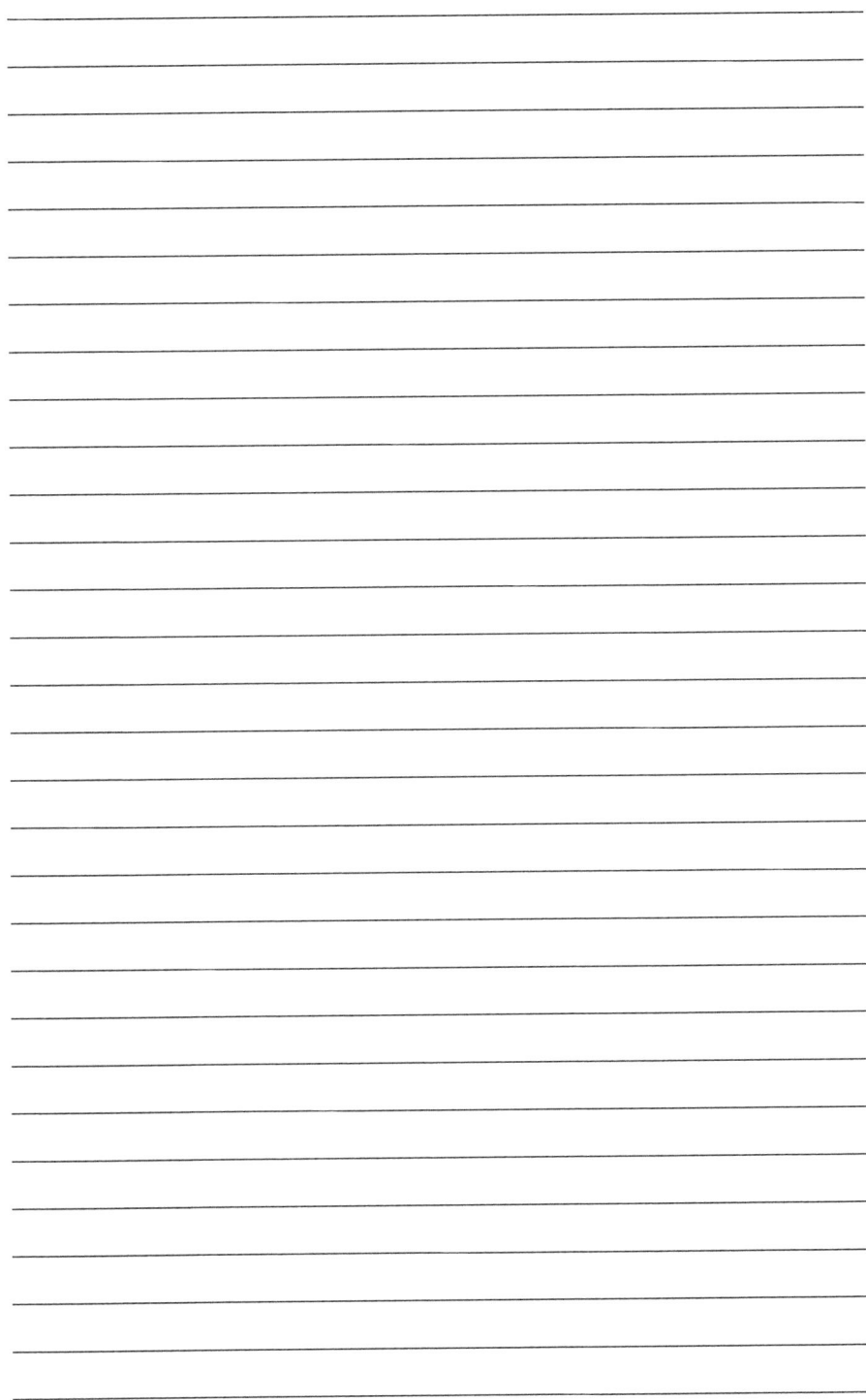

Month_____

INCOME
RENT
GAS
GROCERIES
LEFT FOR BILLS

Bills

EXPENSE	DUE	AMOUNT	PAID	BALANCE LEFT

NOTES

Month_____

Bills

INCOME
RENT
GAS
GROCERIES
LEFT FOR BILLS

EXPENSE	DUE	AMOUNT	PAID	BALANCE LEFT

NOTES

Priority Expenses for the month

- [ ]
- [ ]
- [ ]
- [ ]
- [ ]
- [ ]
- [ ]
- [ ]
- [ ]
- [ ]

- [ ]
- [ ]
- [ ]
- [ ]
- [ ]
- [ ]
- [ ]
- [ ]
- [ ]
- [ ]

APPOINTMENTS

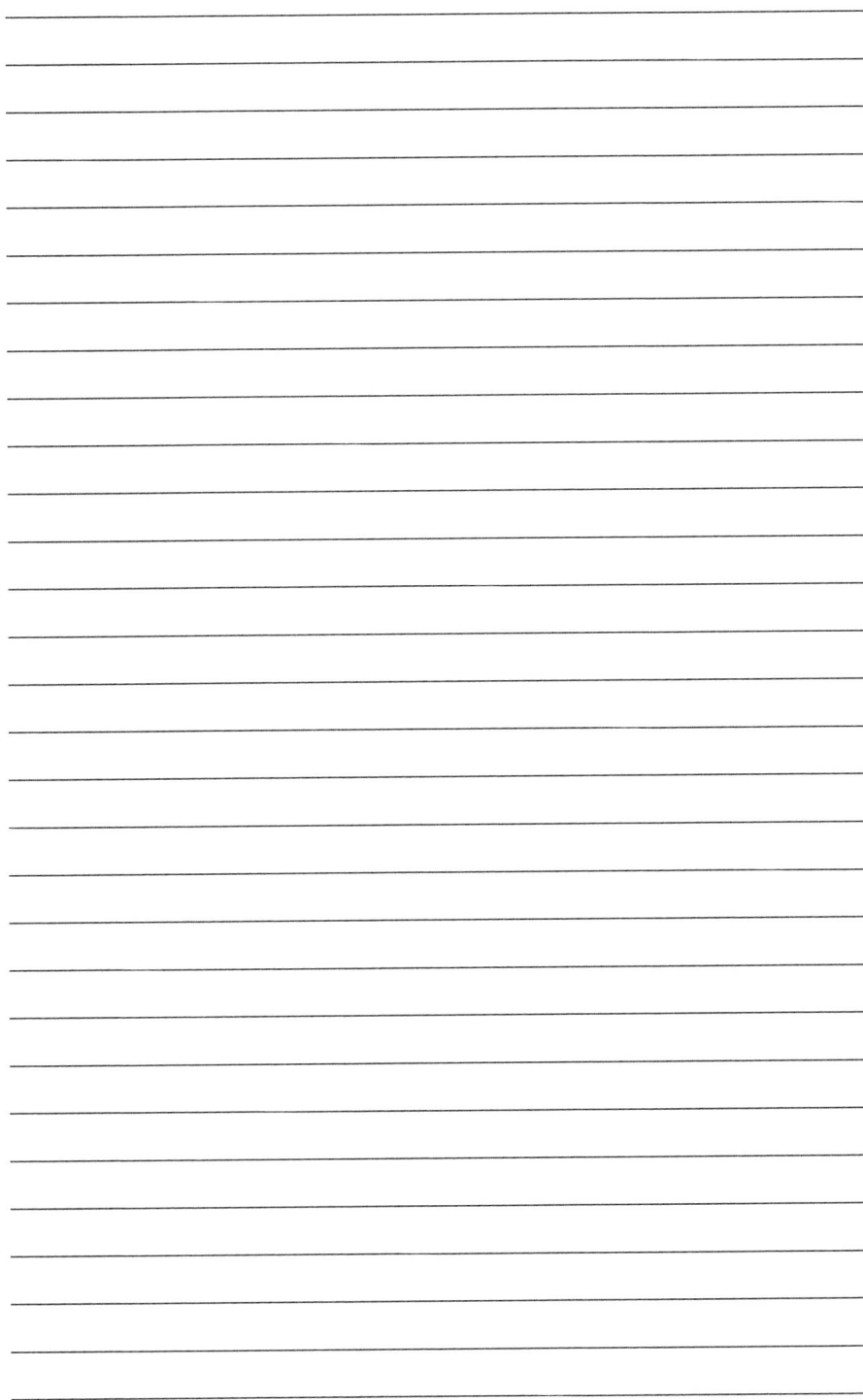

Month_____

Bills

INCOME
RENT
GAS
GROCERIES
LEFT FOR BILLS

EXPENSE	DUE	AMOUNT	PAID	BALANCE LEFT

NOTES

Month_____

Bills

INCOME
RENT
GAS
GROCERIES
LEFT FOR BILLS

EXPENSE	DUE	AMOUNT	PAID	BALANCE LEFT

NOTES

Priority Expenses for the month

- [ ] ....
- [ ] ....
- [ ] ....
- [ ] ....
- [ ] ....
- [ ] ....
- [ ] ....
- [ ] ....
- [ ] ....
- [ ]

- [ ] ....
- [ ] ....
- [ ] ....
- [ ] ....
- [ ] ....
- [ ] ....
- [ ] ....
- [ ] ....
- [ ] ....
- [ ]

APPOINTMENTS

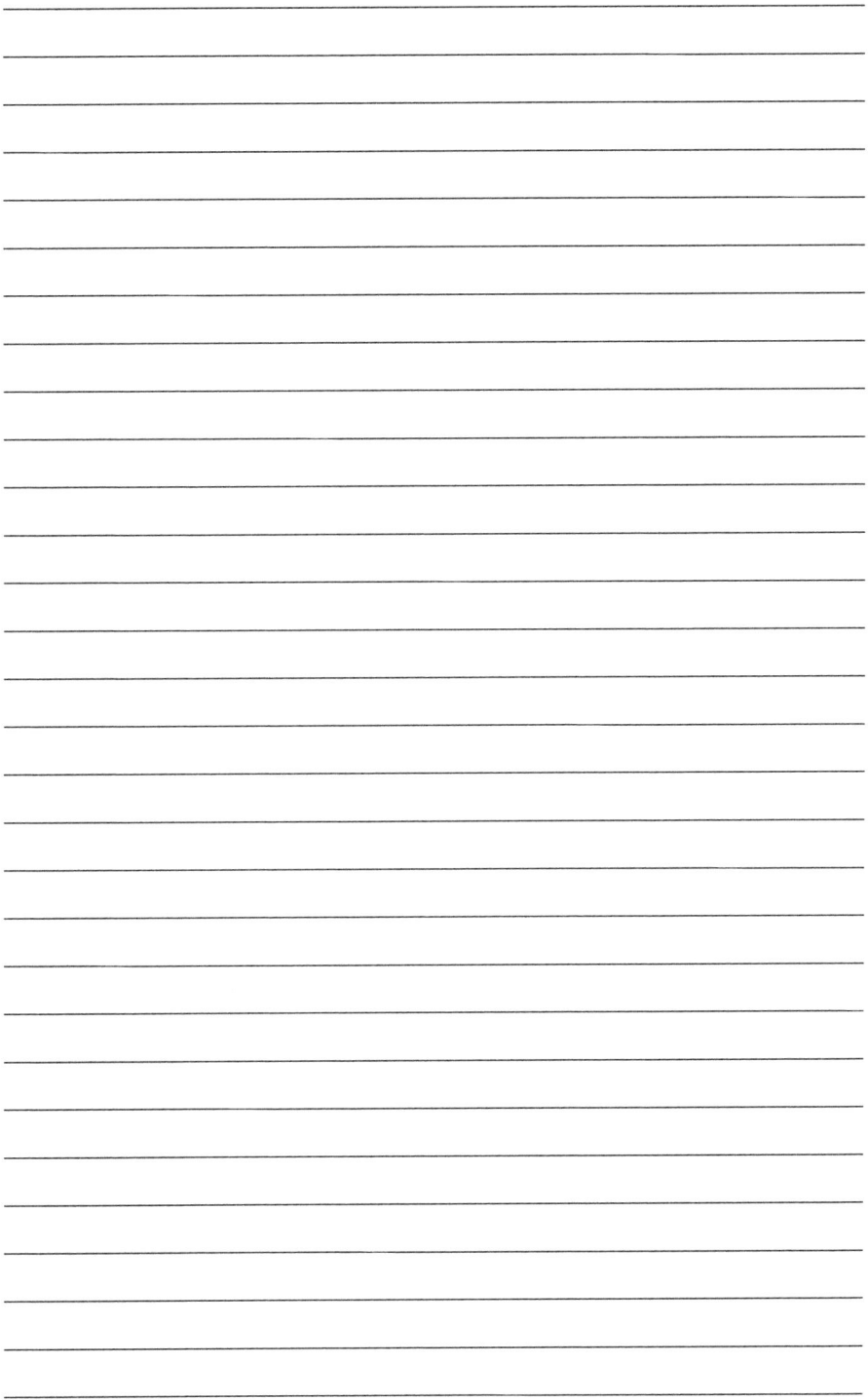

Month_____

Bills

INCOME
RENT
GAS
GROCERIES
LEFT FOR BILLS

EXPENSE	DUE	AMOUNT	PAID	BALANCE LEFT

NOTES

Month_____

Bills

INCOME
RENT
GAS
GROCERIES
LEFT FOR BILLS

EXPENSE	DUE	AMOUNT	PAID	BALANCE LEFT

NOTES

Priority Expenses for the month

- [ ]
- [ ]
- [ ]
- [ ]
- [ ]
- [ ]
- [ ]
- [ ]
- [ ]
- [ ]

- [ ]
- [ ]
- [ ]
- [ ]
- [ ]
- [ ]
- [ ]
- [ ]
- [ ]
- [ ]

APPOINTMENTS

Month_____

Bills

INCOME
RENT
GAS
GROCERIES
LEFT FOR BILLS

EXPENSE	DUE	AMOUNT	PAID	BALANCE LEFT

NOTES

Month_____

Bills

INCOME
RENT
GAS
GROCERIES
LEFT FOR BILLS

EXPENSE	DUE	AMOUNT	PAID	BALANCE LEFT

NOTES

Priority Expenses for the month

- [ ]
- [ ]
- [ ]
- [ ]
- [ ]
- [ ]
- [ ]
- [ ]
- [ ]
- [ ]

- [ ]
- [ ]
- [ ]
- [ ]
- [ ]
- [ ]
- [ ]
- [ ]
- [ ]
- [ ]

APPOINTMENTS

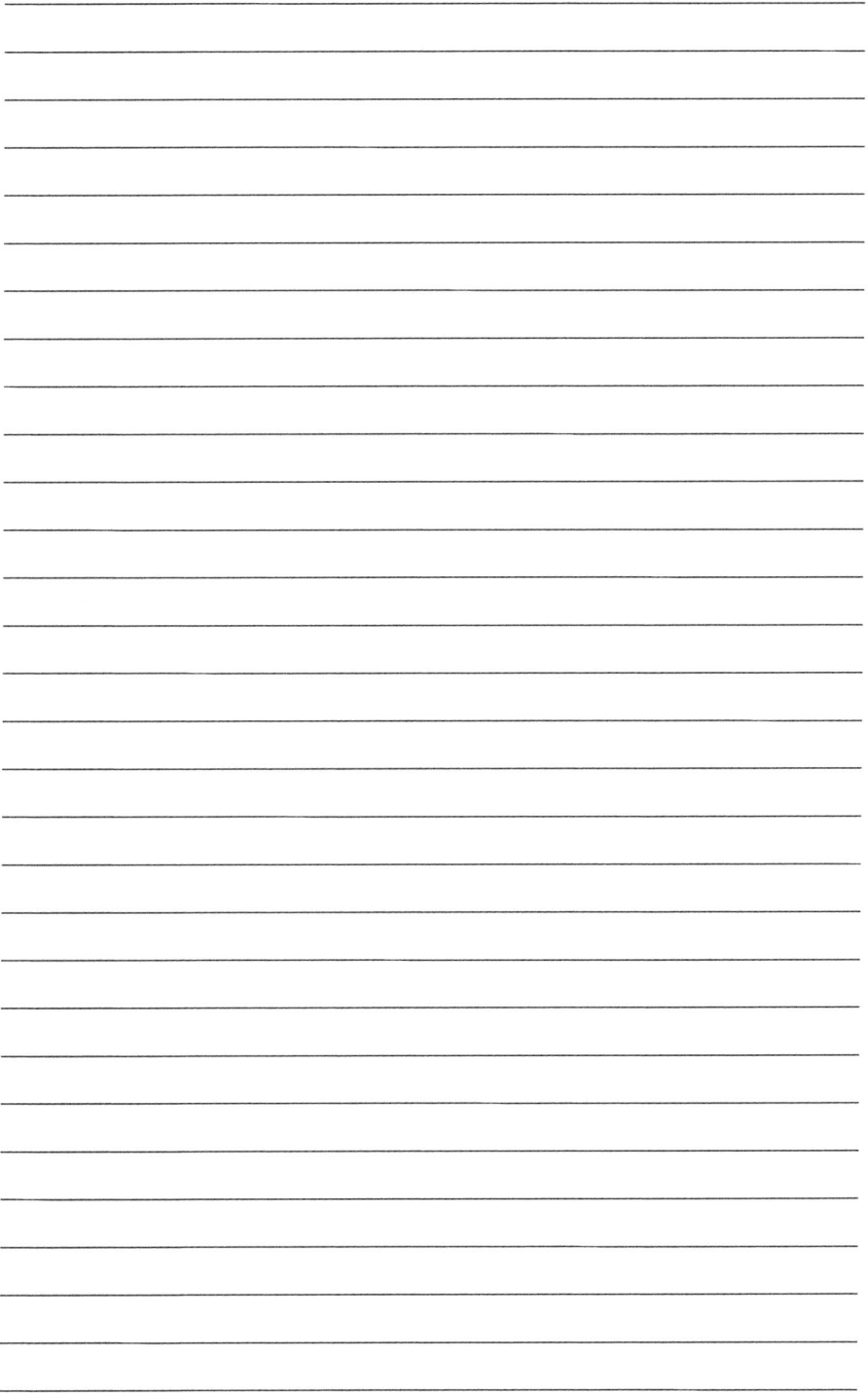

Month_____

Bills

INCOME
RENT
GAS
GROCERIES
LEFT FOR BILLS

EXPENSE	DUE	AMOUNT	PAID	BALANCE LEFT

NOTES

Month_____

Bills

INCOME
RENT
GAS
GROCERIES
LEFT FOR BILLS

EXPENSE	DUE	AMOUNT	PAID	BALANCE LEFT

NOTES

Priority Expenses for the month

- ☐ ....
- ☐ ....
- ☐ ....
- ☐ ....
- ☐ ....
- ☐ ....
- ☐ ....
- ☐ ....
- ☐ ....
- ☐

- ☐ ....
- ☐ ....
- ☐ ....
- ☐ ....
- ☐ ....
- ☐ ....
- ☐ ....
- ☐ ....
- ☐ ....
- ☐

APPOINTMENTS

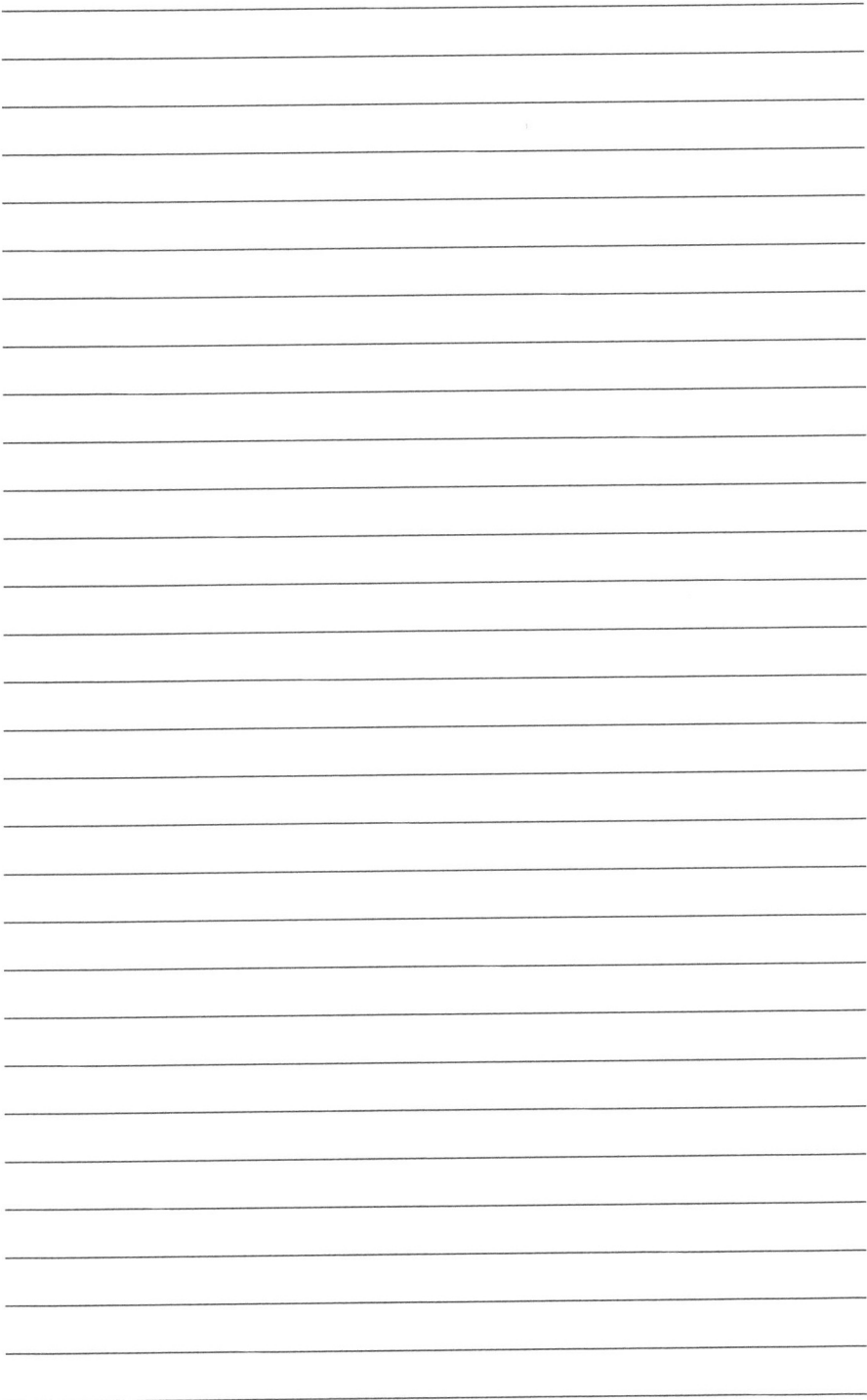

Month_____

Bills

INCOME
RENT
GAS
GROCERIES
LEFT FOR BILLS

EXPENSE	DUE	AMOUNT	PAID	BALANCE LEFT

NOTES

Month_____

Bills

INCOME
RENT
GAS
GROCERIES
LEFT FOR BILLS

EXPENSE	DUE	AMOUNT	PAID	BALANCE LEFT

NOTES

Priority Expenses for the month

- [ ]
- [ ]
- [ ]
- [ ]
- [ ]
- [ ]
- [ ]
- [ ]
- [ ]
- [ ]

- [ ]
- [ ]
- [ ]
- [ ]
- [ ]
- [ ]
- [ ]
- [ ]
- [ ]
- [ ]

APPOINTMENTS

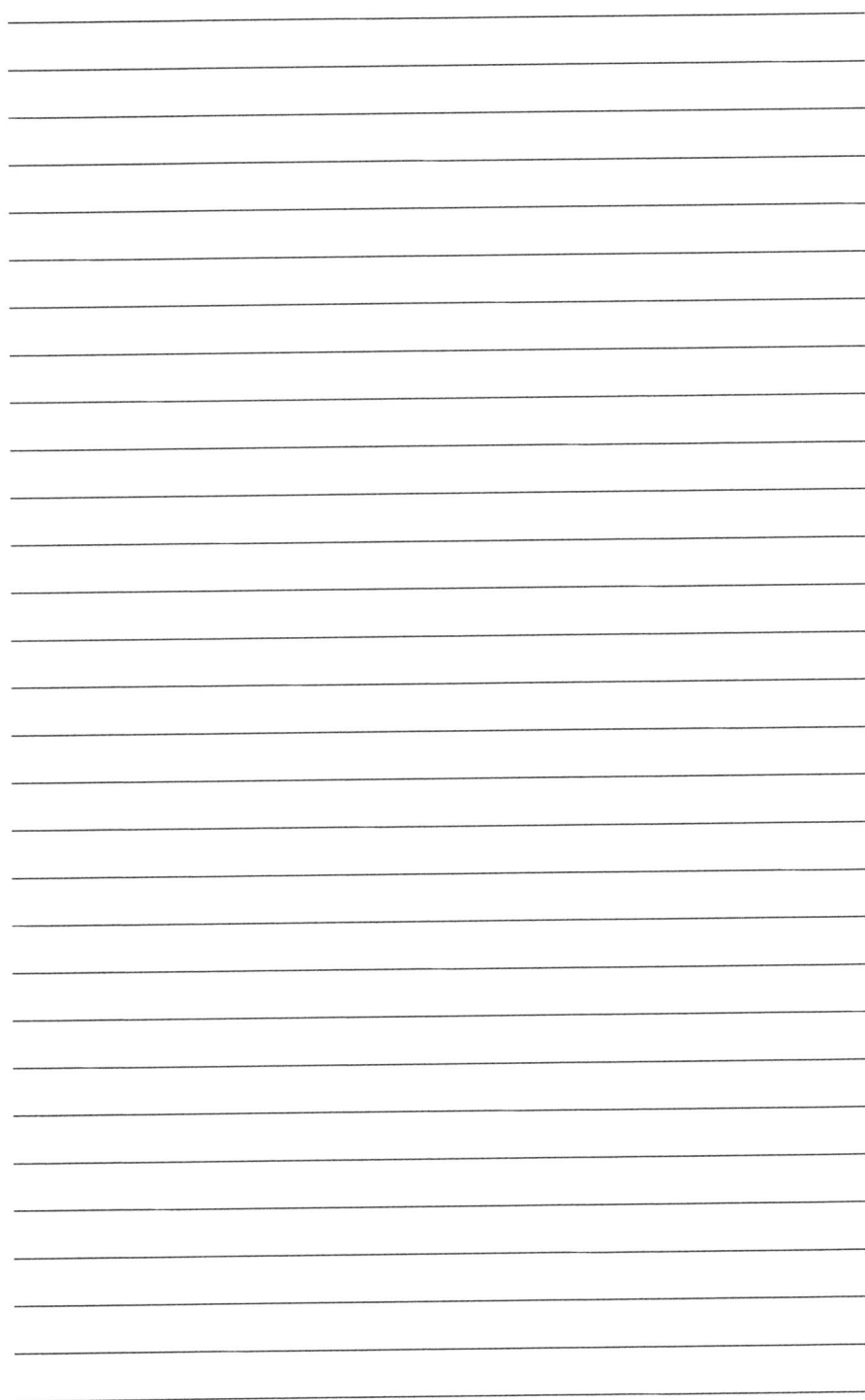

Month_____

Bills

INCOME
RENT
GAS
GROCERIES
LEFT FOR BILLS

EXPENSE	DUE	AMOUNT	PAID	BALANCE LEFT

NOTES

Month_____

INCOME
RENT
GAS
GROCERIES
LEFT FOR BILLS

Bills

EXPENSE	DUE	AMOUNT	PAID	BALANCE LEFT

NOTES

Priority Expenses for the month

- [ ]
- [ ]
- [ ]
- [ ]
- [ ]
- [ ]
- [ ]
- [ ]
- [ ]
- [ ]

- [ ]
- [ ]
- [ ]
- [ ]
- [ ]
- [ ]
- [ ]
- [ ]
- [ ]
- [ ]

APPOINTMENTS

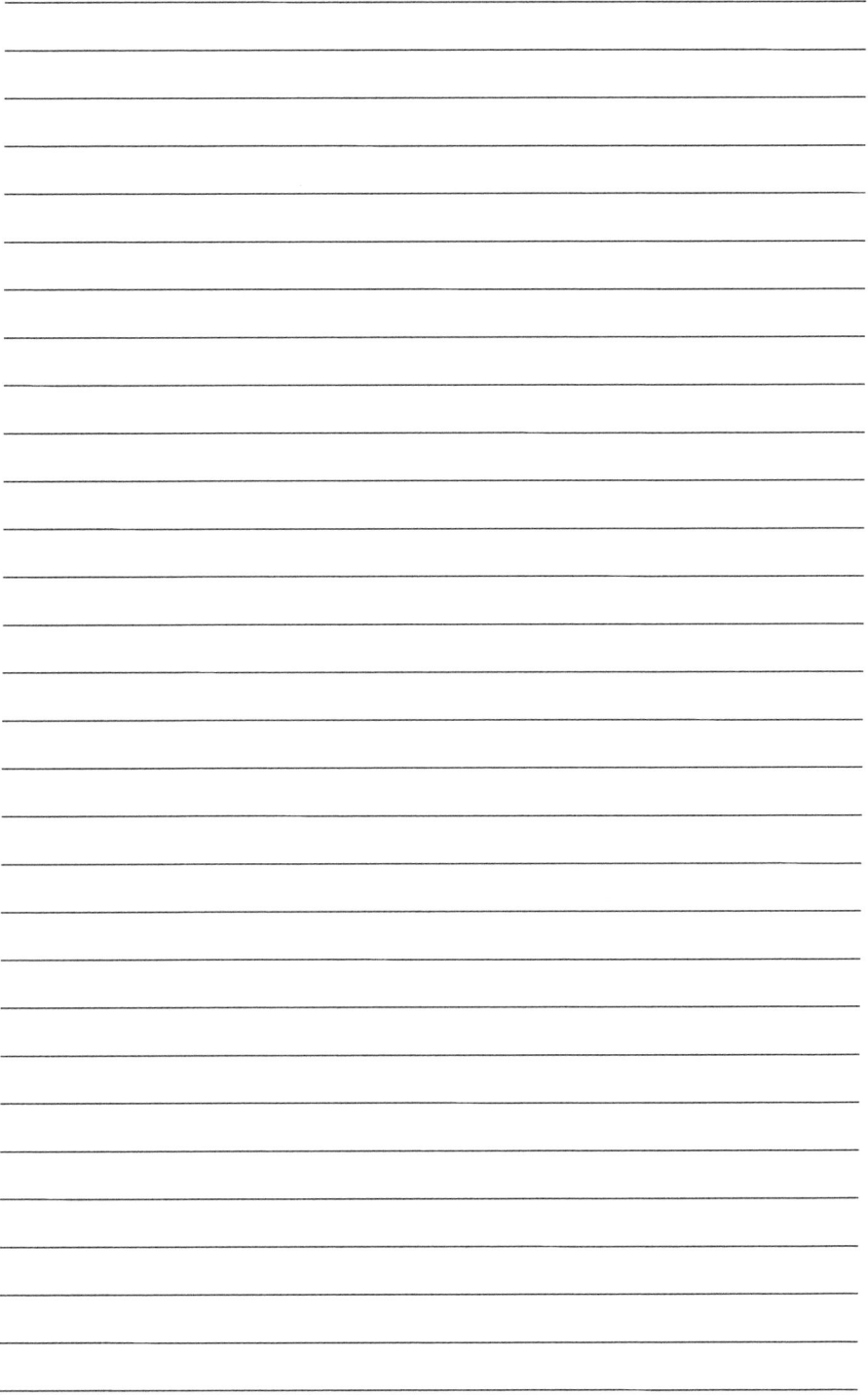

Month_____

Bills

INCOME
RENT
GAS
GROCERIES
LEFT FOR BILLS

EXPENSE	DUE	AMOUNT	PAID	BALANCE LEFT

NOTES

Month_____

Bills

INCOME
RENT
GAS
GROCERIES
LEFT FOR BILLS

EXPENSE	DUE	AMOUNT	PAID	BALANCE LEFT

NOTES

Month_____

Bills

INCOME
RENT
GAS
GROCERIES
LEFT FOR BILLS

EXPENSE	DUE	AMOUNT	PAID	BALANCE LEFT

NOTES

Month_____

Bills

INCOME
RENT
GAS
GROCERIES
LEFT FOR BILLS

EXPENSE	DUE	AMOUNT	PAID	BALANCE LEFT

NOTES

Priority Expenses for the month

- [ ]
- [ ]
- [ ]
- [ ]
- [ ]
- [ ]
- [ ]
- [ ]
- [ ]
- [ ]

- [ ]
- [ ]
- [ ]
- [ ]
- [ ]
- [ ]
- [ ]
- [ ]
- [ ]
- [ ]

APPOINTMENTS

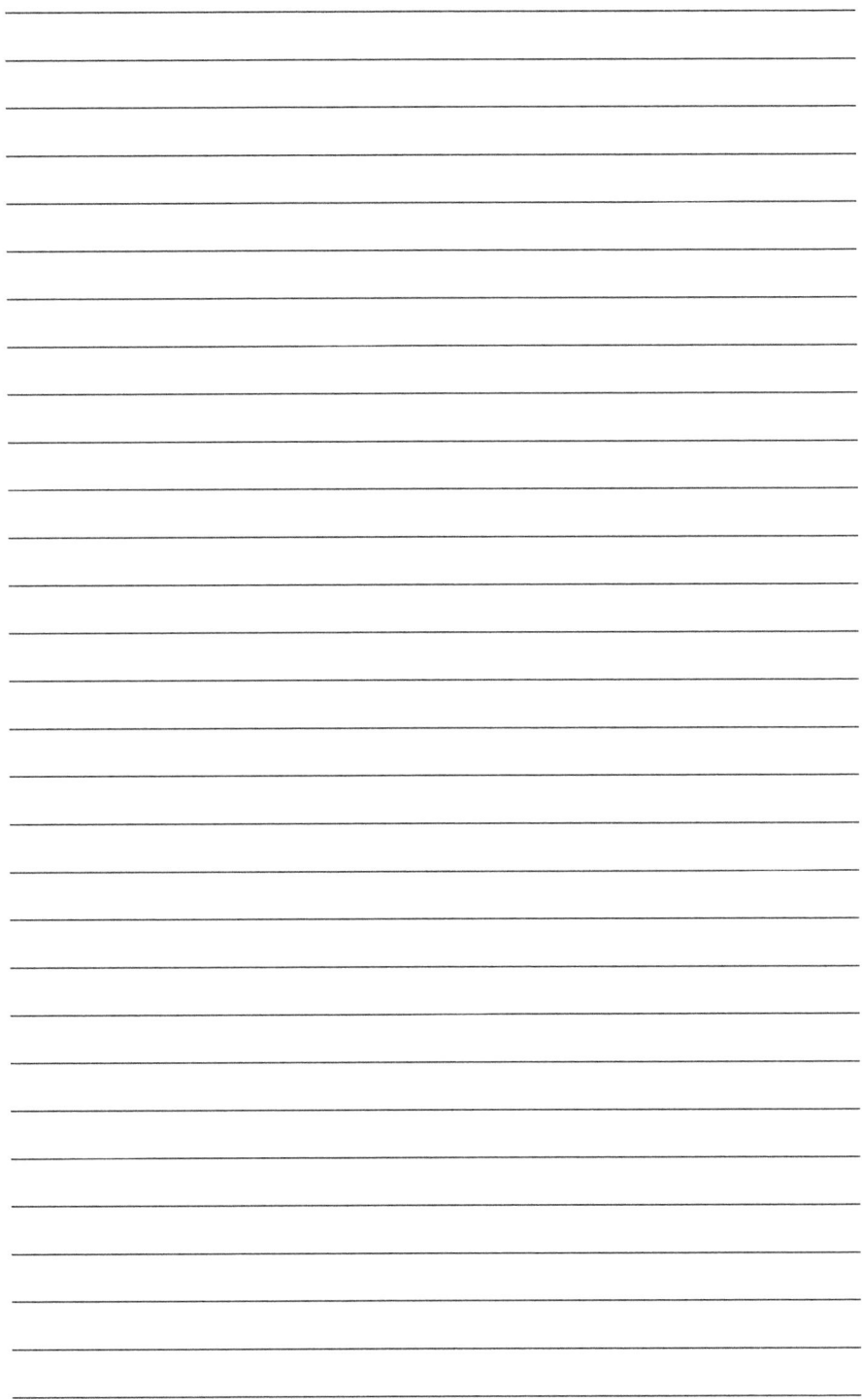

Month_____

Bills

INCOME
RENT
GAS
GROCERIES
LEFT FOR BILLS

EXPENSE	DUE	AMOUNT	PAID	BALANCE LEFT

NOTES

Month_____

INCOME
RENT
GAS
GROCERIES
LEFT FOR BILLS

Bills

EXPENSE	DUE	AMOUNT	PAID	BALANCE LEFT

NOTES

Priority Expenses for the month

- [ ]
- [ ]
- [ ]
- [ ]
- [ ]
- [ ]
- [ ]
- [ ]
- [ ]
- [ ]

- [ ]
- [ ]
- [ ]
- [ ]
- [ ]
- [ ]
- [ ]
- [ ]
- [ ]
- [ ]

APPOINTMENTS

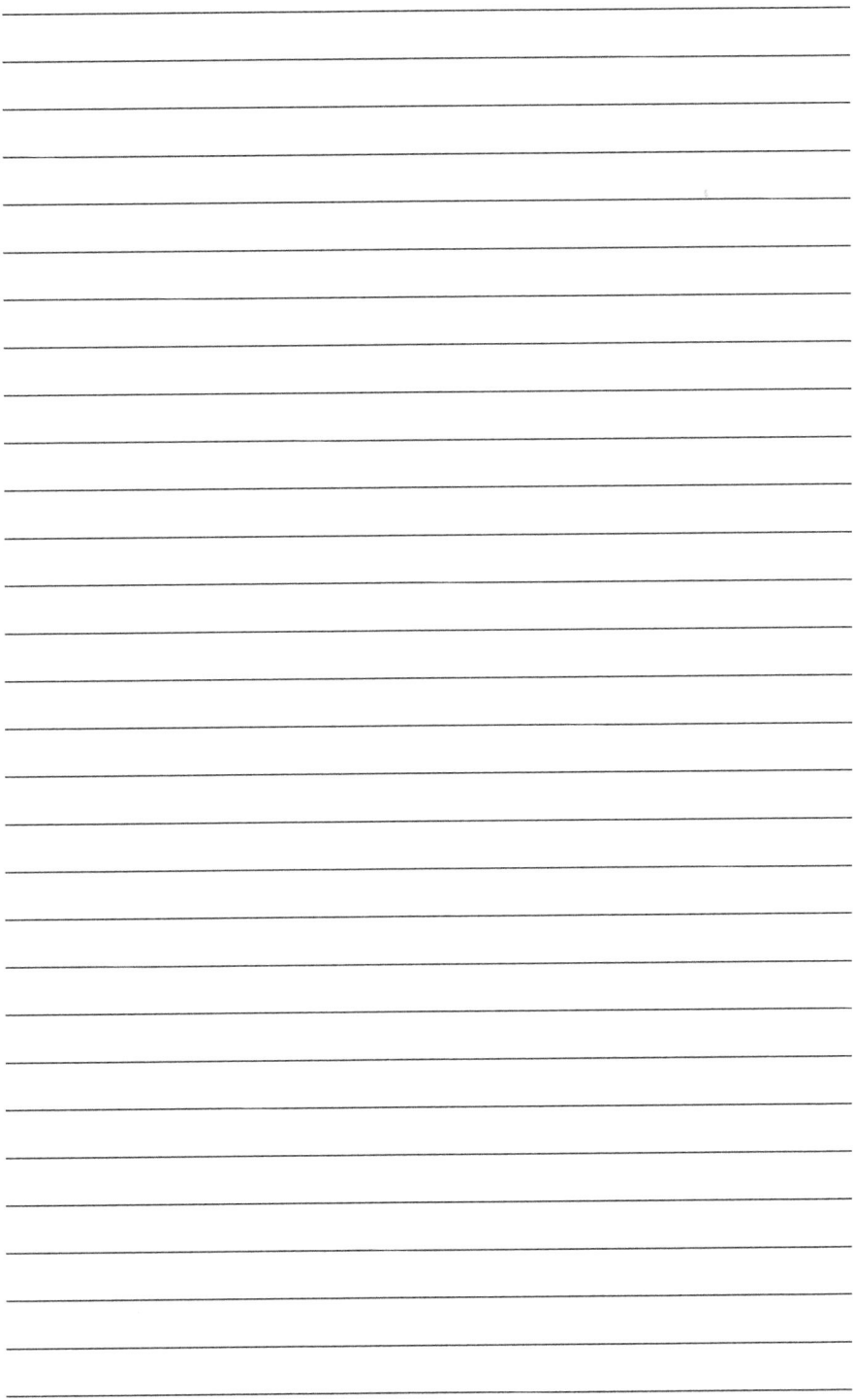

Month_____

Bills

INCOME
RENT
GAS
GROCERIES
LEFT FOR BILLS

EXPENSE	DUE	AMOUNT	PAID	BALANCE LEFT

NOTES

Month_____

Bills

INCOME
RENT
GAS
GROCERIES
LEFT FOR BILLS

EXPENSE	DUE	AMOUNT	PAID	BALANCE LEFT

NOTES

Priority Expenses for the month

- [ ]
- [ ]
- [ ]
- [ ]
- [ ]
- [ ]
- [ ]
- [ ]
- [ ]
- [ ]

- [ ]
- [ ]
- [ ]
- [ ]
- [ ]
- [ ]
- [ ]
- [ ]
- [ ]
- [ ]

APPOINTMENTS

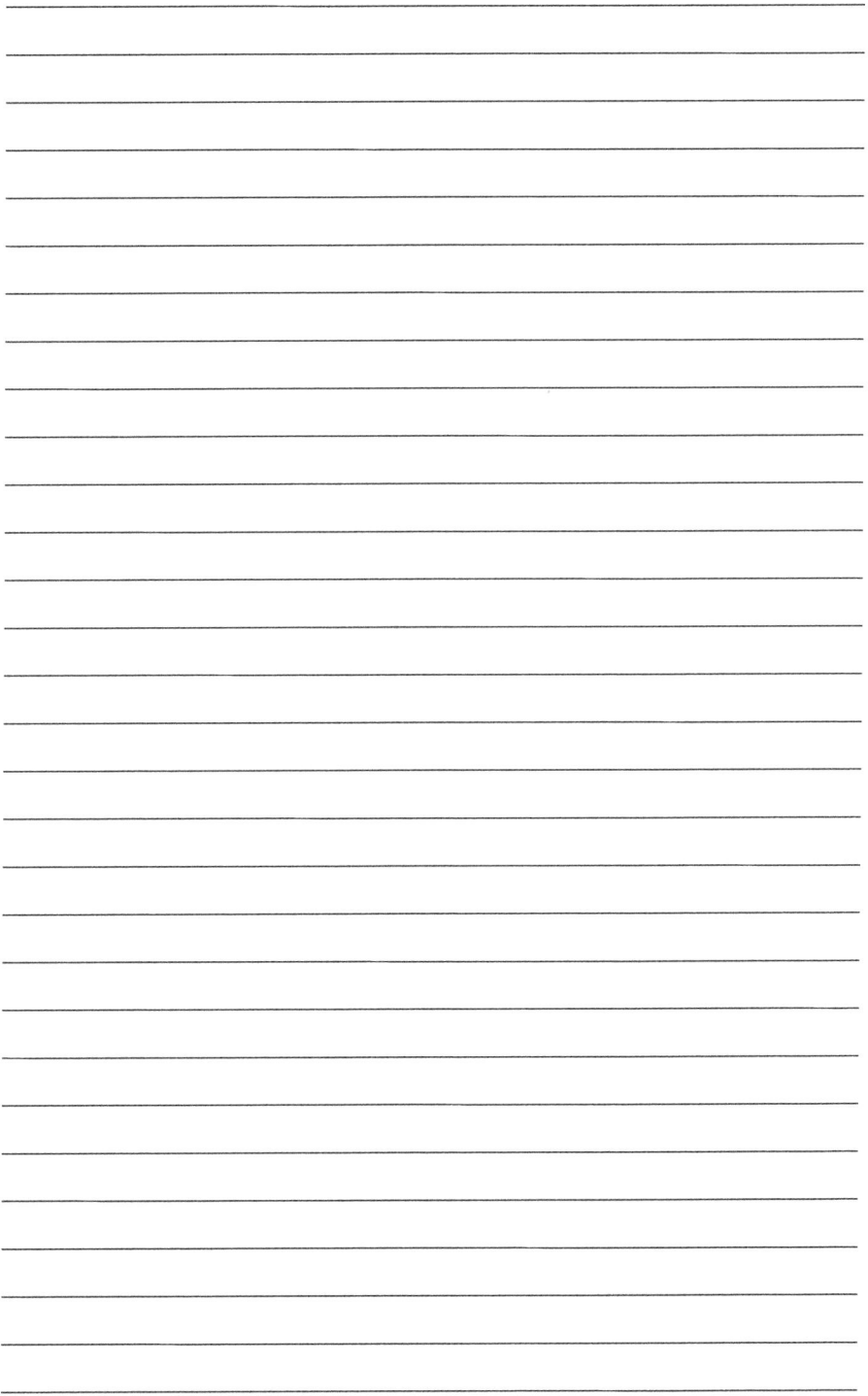

Month_____

Bills

INCOME
RENT
GAS
GROCERIES
LEFT FOR BILLS

EXPENSE	DUE	AMOUNT	PAID	BALANCE LEFT

NOTES

Month_____

Bills

INCOME
RENT
GAS
GROCERIES
LEFT FOR BILLS

EXPENSE	DUE	AMOUNT	PAID	BALANCE LEFT

NOTES

Priority Expenses for the month

- ☐
- ☐
- ☐
- ☐
- ☐
- ☐
- ☐
- ☐
- ☐
- ☐

- ☐
- ☐
- ☐
- ☐
- ☐
- ☐
- ☐
- ☐
- ☐
- ☐

APPOINTMENTS

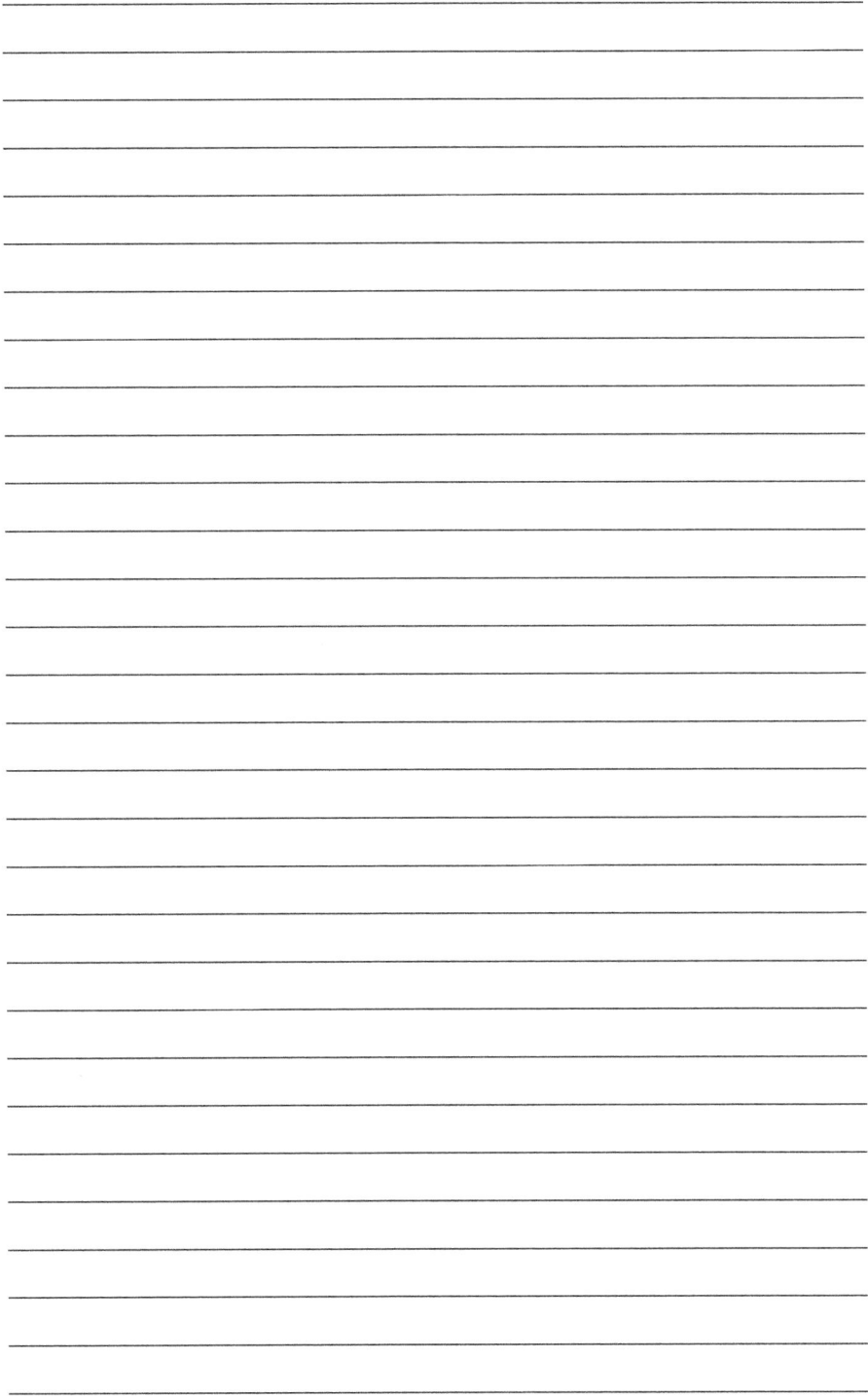

Month_____

Bills

EXPENSE	DUE	AMOUNT	PAID	BALANCE LEFT

NOTES

Month_____

Bills

INCOME
RENT
GAS
GROCERIES
LEFT FOR BILLS

EXPENSE	DUE	AMOUNT	PAID	BALANCE LEFT

NOTES

Priority Expenses for the month

- [ ]
- [ ]
- [ ]
- [ ]
- [ ]
- [ ]
- [ ]
- [ ]
- [ ]
- [ ]

- [ ]
- [ ]
- [ ]
- [ ]
- [ ]
- [ ]
- [ ]
- [ ]
- [ ]
- [ ]

APPOINTMENTS

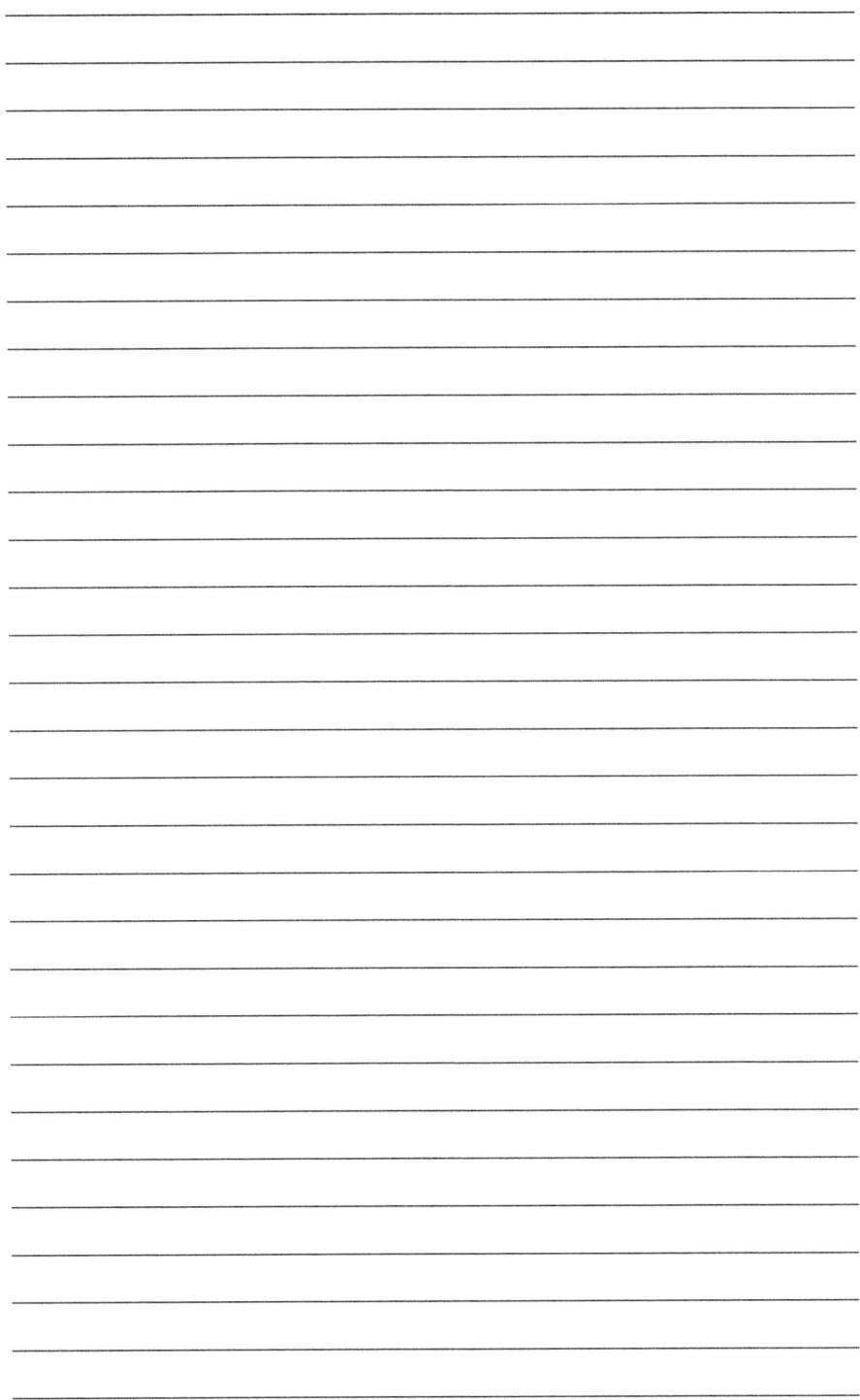

Month_____

Bills

INCOME
RENT
GAS
GROCERIES
LEFT FOR BILLS

EXPENSE	DUE	AMOUNT	PAID	BALANCE LEFT

NOTES

Month_____

Bills

INCOME
RENT
GAS
GROCERIES
LEFT FOR BILLS

EXPENSE	DUE	AMOUNT	PAID	BALANCE LEFT

NOTES

www.ingramcontent.com/pod-product-compliance
Lightning Source LLC
Chambersburg PA
CBHW081335090426
42737CB00017B/3157